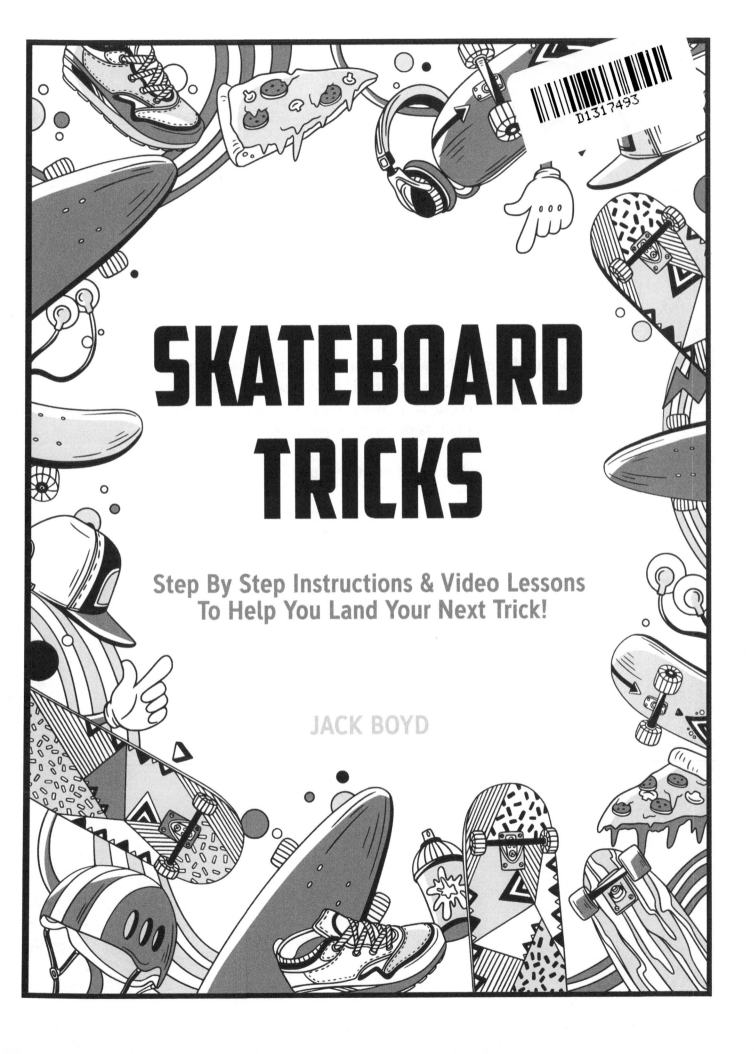

SKATEBOARD TRICKS

Step By Step Instructions & Video Lessons
To Help You Land Your Next Trick!

JACK BOYD

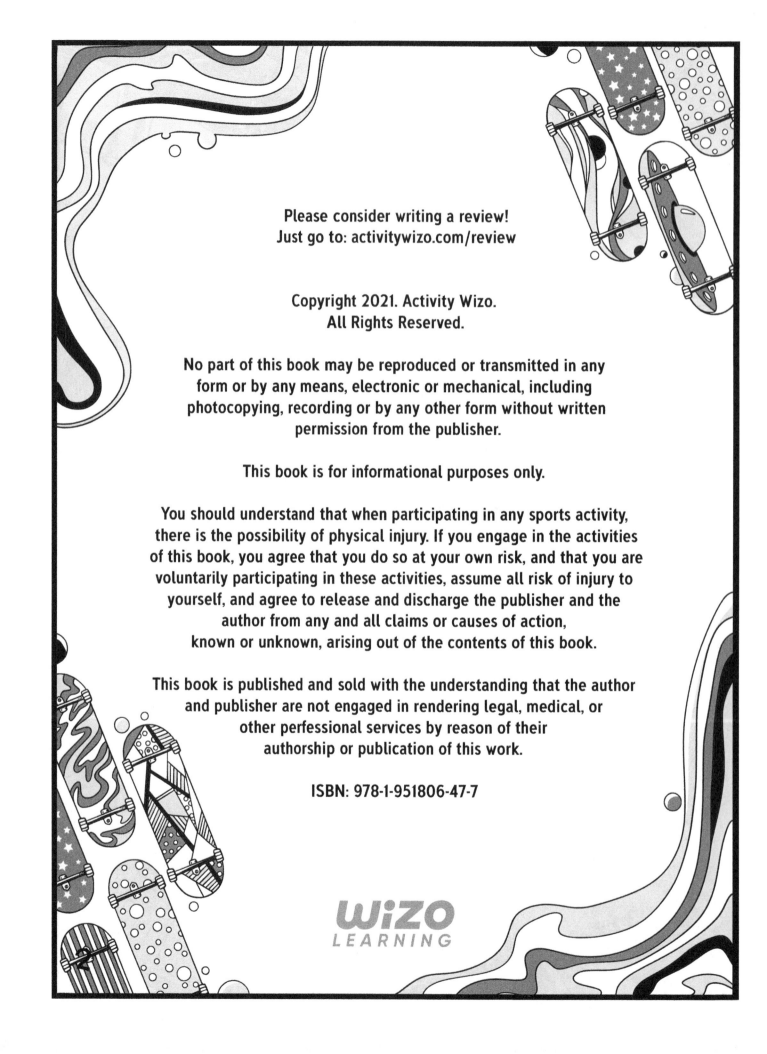

WiZO
LEARNING

TABLE OF CONTENTS

FREE BONUS VIDEOS		3
CHAPTER 1:	FLIP TRICKS	7
CHAPTER 2:	GRAB TRICKS	17
CHAPTER 3:	AIR TRICKS	31
CHAPTER 4:	SLIDE TRICKS	43
CHAPTER 5:	RAMP TRICKS	65

Chapter 1
Flip Tricks

Kickflip

Step 1: Get ready to snap an ollie. Put pressure on your back foot and place your front foot so that it's just below the front bolts.

Step 2: Bend your knees and snap your tail. Bring your front foot toward the nose of your board as you jump up.

Step 3: Give the nose a quick flick with your front foot. Make sure to keep your shoulders straight.

Step 4: Stay centered with your feet in the landing position as your board flips beneath you. You got this!

Step 5: Catch the board with your feet.

Step 6: Roll away.

Hard Flip

Step 1: Don't let the name scare you! A hardflip is just a combination of a frontside 180 ollie with a kickflip. Set up with your feet in the ollie position.

Step 2: Bend down and get ready to snap your tail.

Step 3: Pop your back foot like you're doing a frontside 180 ollie. Bring your front foot up and flick it like a kickflip but more sideways.

Step 4: You need more airtime than a regular kickflip. Jump up high while you kick your back and front foot in opposite directions.

Step 5: Catch the board with your feet.

Step 6: Land and roll away. You did it!

Heelflip

Step 1: Get your feet into the ollie position with your front foot more toward the inside edge of your board.

Step 2: Pop your tail, jump up, and kick your front foot forwards.

Step 3: As your board comes up, flip the board with your heel. You're going to have to give it a good kick!

Step 4: Stay centered over your board with your feet in the landing position.

Step 5: Let your board touch your feet.

Step 6: Stick the landing and roll away. Woo hoo!

Varial Heelflip

Step 1: A varial heelflip combines a heelflip with a backside shove it. Get your feet into the ollie position with your back heel hanging off.

Step 2: Pop your tail so that your board turns backside.

Step 3: Kick your front foot with your heel.

Step 4: Stay above your board as it flips and spins 180 degrees backside.

Step 5: Keep your weight centered.

Step 6: Stomp the landing and roll away!

Chapter 2
Grab Tricks

Indy Grab

Step 1: Whether you're ollieing into one on a flat surface or in a skatepark bowl, you can do an indy grab anywhere! Get into the ollie position.

Step 2: Bend your knees and pop an ollie. You're going to need some air, so give it a good snap.

Step 3: Let your board come up to your hand instead of leaning down to grab it.

Step 4: Hold on and fly.

Step 5: Let go of your board.

Step 6: Land it and get ready for your next trick!

Early Grab 360

Step 1: You're going to need a bit of a launch for this one, so it's best tried off of a jump at a skatepark. Bend your knees with a good amount of speed.

Step 2: Set up like you're going to do a frontside 180 ollie.

Step 3: Let the board come up to your hand as the rest of your body is turning frontside.

Step 4: Use your leading arm to help spin you around a full 360 degrees.

Step 5: Spot your landing, making sure you've made a full rotation.

Step 6: Bend your knees to absorb the impact and keep on rolling!

Tail Grab

Step 1: Bend those knees and get ready to ollie high!

Step 2: After you ollie, bring up your back hand down behind you.

Step 3: Kick your front forward to level out your board and grab the tail.

Step 4: Let go of your board.

Step 5: Touch down on your wheels.

Step 6: Ride away!

Nose Grab

Step 1: Get your feet ready in the ollie position.

Step 2: Give your tail a crack and jump up while keeping your leading hand a bit lower than usual.

Step 3: Let the nose of your board come up into your hand.

Step 4: Release your board.

Step 5: Keep your weight centered.

Step 6: Land it!

Stalefish Grab

Step 1: This is a great one to try on a ramp or at the skatepark. Set up like you're going to do a frontside ollie.

Step 2: As you go up the transition, put pressure on your back foot.

Step 3: Pop an ollie by snapping your tail or bonking your wheels off the coping.

Step 4: Suck your legs up and let your board come up to your trailing hand.

Step 5: Let go of your skateboard and touch down on the wall.

Step 6: Land and get ready for your next rad trick!

Superman Grab

Step 1: To fly like a superhero, find a transition at your skatepark that has a nice flat landing. Ride up with a good amount of speed.

Step 2: Pop off the top and lift your feet off your board.

Step 3: Grab the nose with both hands.

Step 4: Extend your legs.

Step 5: Bring your legs back to your board while still holding on.

Step 6: Let go and land. Woo hoo!

Chapter 3
Air Tricks

Method Air

Step 1: If you have your backside airs down, you're ready for a method air. Go up a ramp with your knees bent.

Step 2: Bring your leading hand down toward your board.

Step 3: Pop off the top like you're doing an ollie.

Step 4: Grab your board backside behind your heel and pull up.

Step 5: Let go of your board.

Step 6: Set your wheels down and ride away.

Rocket Air

Step 1 : Ride up the ramp with your knees bent and leading hand ready to grab your board.

Step 2: As you lift off the top, bring the front of your board into your leading hand.

Step 3: Turn your board and body backside.

Step 4: Take the other hand and grab the front and bring your front foot down to your tail.

Step 5: Bring your front foot back to the top of your board and let go.

Step 6: Touch your wheels down and ride away.

Backside Air

Step 1: Ride up the ramp with your knees bent.

Step 2: Get your front hand ready to grab your board.

Step 3: Pop your tail or bonk your wheels off the lip.

Step 4: Grab the nose of your board with your leading hand.

Step 5: Release your board.

Step 6: Ride away!

Judo Air

Step 1: Ride up the ramp like you're going to do a backside air.

Step 2: Pop off the lip and scoop your board into your leading hand.

Step 3: Take your front foot off and give it your biggest ninja kick!

Step 4: Put your front foot back on your board.

Step 5: Let go of your board.

Step 6: Get ready for your next trick.

Christ Air

Step 1: Named after '80s vert skater Christian Hosoi, this is a crowd-pleaser! Set up for a backside air.

Step 2: Pop off the lip and grab the top of your board with your front hand.

Step 3: Extend your legs and body like the letter T.

Step 4: Put your board back under your feet.

Step 5: Set your wheels down.

Step 6: Ride away!

Chapter 4
Slide Tricks

BS Bluntslide

Step 1: Approach the ledge with your knees bent and feet ready to ollie.

Step 2: Pop your board up and focus on keeping your weight on your back foot.

Step 3: Turn your board and body and bring your tail down on the top.

Step 4: Put pressure on your back foot, lean back, and slide.

Step 5: When you get to the end, pop off by putting pressure on your back foot and turning backside.

Step 6: Stick your landing.

FS Lipslide

Step 1: Approach the ledge like you're going to pop a frontside 180 ollie.

Step 2: Snap your tail and start turning frontside.

Step 3: Make sure you pop high enough above the ledge to get your board over it.

Step 4: Land on your board and lean back so that you slide.

Step 5: Put pressure on your back foot.

Step 6: When you're at the end, press on your back foot, turn your board, and land it. Well done!

BS Lipslide

Step 1: Bend your knees and approach the ledge like you're going to do a backside 180 ollie.

Step 2: Pull up your legs and start turning in the air.

Step 3: Press down on your back foot and lock your board onto the top.

Step 4: Keep your weight toward your toes just enough for your board to slide.

Step 5: When you get to the end press on your back foot and turn frontside.

Step 6: Stay centered over your board and roll away.

FS Tailslide

Step 1: Approach the ledge like you're going to do a frontside 180 ollie.

Step 2: Pop an ollie and start turning frontside while keeping your weight on your back foot.

Step 3: When your back wheels are above the ledge, press down on your back foot.

Step 4: Lock your tail on the edge, lean back, and slide.

Step 5: When you get to the end of your slide, pop your tail off and turn your board.

Step 6: Land it and ride away!

BS Tailslide

Step 1: Approach the ledge parallel and set up like you're going to do a backside 180 ollie.

Step 2: Ollie and start turning backside keeping your weight on your back foot.

Step 3: When your back foot clears the top of the ledge, press down on it.

Step 4: Put all of your weight on your back foot and slide on your tail.

Step 5: When you get to the end, press on your back foot and pop off backside.

Step 6: Let your wheels touch down. Nice job!

FS Boardslide

Step 1: Approach the ledge or flatbar with a decent amount of speed.

Step 2: Ollie like you're going to do a backside 180.

Step 3: Make sure you get enough height to get all of your wheels over the top.

Step 4: Keep centered over your board as it slides.

Step 5: Turn off the end frontside.

Step 6: Land it and keep on rolling.

BS Boardslide

Step 1: Approach the ledge or flat bar with a good amount of speed.

Step 2: Pop your board like you're going to do a frontside 180 ollie.

Step 3: Make sure you get enough height so that all four wheels get above what you want to slide.

Step 4: Touch your board down.

Step 5: Lean back as you slide.

Step 6: Turn off the end backside and ride away.

FS Noseslide

Step 1: Approach the object with your front foot more toward the bolts.

Step 2: Pop an ollie.

Step 3: Make sure that your front foot slides up to the nose.

Step 4: Turn your board and body and place all your weight on your front foot.

Step 5: Stand up on your front foot and let your nose slide.

Step 6: Turn off the end frontside and ride away.

BS Noseslide

Step 1: Approach the obstacle with your front foot more toward the nose.

Step 2: Snap an ollie and let your front foot come up to the nose.

Step 3: Turn your board and shoulders.

Step 4: Let the nose come down on the obstacle and put most of your weight on your front foot.

Step 5: Lean back and keep pressure on your front foot as you slide.

Step 6: Pop off the end with your nose and turn backside. You did it!

FS Bluntslide

Step 1: Approach the obstacle with a good amount of speed.

Step 2: You're going to need some height, so pop the biggest ollie that you can!

Step 3: Turn your board and body backside.

Step 4: When your back wheels get above the obstacle, press down on your back foot and slide on your tail.

Step 5: When you get to the end, turn your board and body frontside back to your original position.

Step 6: Stick your landing!

Chapter 5
Ramp Tricks

BS Smith Stall

Step 1: Roll up the ramp with your back foot scooted just a bit up on your tail.

Step 2: Approach the lip with enough speed to get to the top.

Step 3: Press on your back foot like you're going to do an axle stall.

Step 4: Lock your back truck, putting pressure on your back heel. Straighten your front leg out.

Step 5: Press on your back toes, ease your back truck over the coping, and roll back down.

BS Feeble Stall

Step 1: Ride up the wall with enough speed to reach the lip.

Step 2: Keep your eyes on the coping as you roll up the transition.

Step 3: As you get close to the top, start turning your body backside.

Step 4: Let your back truck come to rest on the coping.

Step 5: Tap the deck with your front wheels.

Step 6: Put weight on your back foot and turn back into the ramp.

BS Crooked Stall

Step 1: Ride up the wall with your front foot up on the nose of your board.

Step 2: When the nose of your board reaches the coping, press on your toes.

Step 3: Press on your nose and bring your back truck up.

Step 4: Press on your back foot and straighten your board.

Step 5: Press down on your back foot and drop in backward.

Step 6: Roll down the ramp. That wasn't so scary, was it?

BS Disaster

Step 1: Keep your weight centered and roll up the ramp.

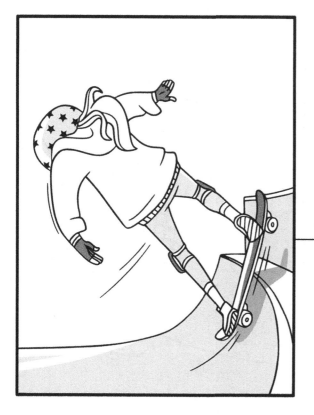

Step 2: As you come to the top, start turning like you would for a backside kickturn.

Step 3: Scoop your board and turn 180, keeping your weight on the back foot.

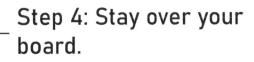

Step 4: Stay over your board.

Step 5: Touch your board down on the top of the ramp.

Step 6: Press on your nose, popping your back wheels over the coping and ride back in.

BS Rock 'n' Roll

Step 1: Pump up the transition with a moderate amount of speed.

Step 2: As your front wheels rise above the lip, press your leg forward and push your board so it slaps down on the deck.

Step 3: Hang there for a moment.

Step 4: Put pressure on your back foot and start turning your shoulders toward the ramp.

Step 5: Swing your front wheels over and do a backside kickturn back in.

Step 6: Ride down the ramp—you did it!

BS Tail Stall

Step 1: Approach the lip backside with your front shoulder a bit more toward the ramp.

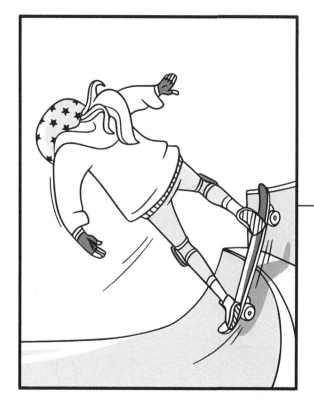

Step 2: Lift your back wheels.

Step 3: Turn your body and board backside.

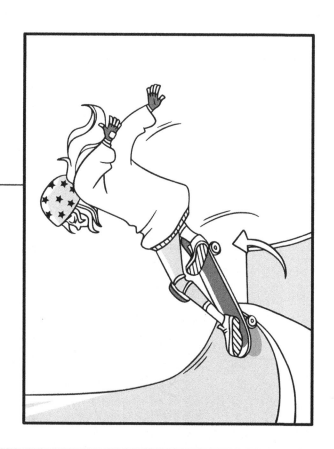

Step 4: Complete the rotation of your board and body.

Step 5: Keep your weight on your back foot as you turn and stand on your tail.

Step 6: Press on your nose and drop back into the ramp.

Axle Drop In

Step 1: Set your trucks on the coping.

Step 2: Put pressure on your back foot and pivot the nose of your board toward the ramp.

Step 3: Pop your tail off the lip, lean forward into the ramp, and ride away.

Made in the USA
Monee, IL
10 December 2021

84719434R00044